BE A MAKER!

MAKER PROJECTS FOR KIDS WHO LOVE

MUSIC

REBECCA SJONGER

CRABTREE
Publishing Company
www.crabtreebooks.com

Crabtree Publishing Company

www.crabtreebooks.com

Author: Rebecca Sjonger

Publishing plan research and development:
Reagan Miller

Editors: Sarah Eason, Harriet McGregor,
Reagan Miller

Proofreaders: Nancy Dickmann, Petrice Custance

Editorial director: Kathy Middleton

Design: Paul Myerscough

Cover design: Emma DeBanks

Photo research: Rachel Blount

**Production coordinator and
Prepress techician:** Tammy McGarr

Print coordinator: Margaret Amy Salter

Consultant: Chris Stone

Production coordinated by Calcium Creative

Photo Credits:

t=Top, bl=Bottom Left, br=Bottom Right

National Music Centre, Calgary, Canada: Evan Rothery: p. 29b;
Shutterstock: Abbitt Photography: p. 18; BasPhoto: p. 14; Christian
Bertrand: p. 23; DiversityStudio: p. 7; Everett Collection: p. 6t; Furtseff:
p. 8; Keith Gentry: p. 16; Sean Pavone: p. 26; Renato Pejkovic: p.
22; Photoff: p. 4; PI: p. 12; Andrea Raffin: p. 25; SJ Travel Photo and
Video: p. 9; Snapgalleria: p. 6b; Olaf Speier: p. 5b; Ronald Sumners: p.
5t; Sydneymills: p. 24; Tudor Photography: pp. 10–11, 20–21, 28, 29t;
Wikimedia Commons: Aconcagua: p. 15; Vince Flango: p. 17; Glogger:
p. 1, 27; Library of Congress/World-Telegram staff photographer: p. 13;
Yamaha: Design Center, Yamaha Motor Europe NV: p. 19.

Cover: Tudor Photography.

Library and Archives Canada Cataloguing in Publication

Sjonger, Rebecca, author
        Maker projects for kids who love music / Rebecca Sjonger.

(Be a maker!)
Includes index.
Issued in print and electronic formats.
ISBN 978-0-7787-2252-6 (hardcover).--
ISBN 978-0-7787-2264-9 (paperback).--
ISBN 978-1-4271-1720-5 (html)

        1. Musical instruments--Juvenile literature. 2. Music--Juve-
nile literature. I. Title.

ML460.S625 2016   j784.19   C2015-907926-8
                                                        C2015-907927-6

Library of Congress Cataloging-in-Publication Data

Names: Sjonger, Rebecca.
Title: Maker projects for kids who love music / Rebecca Sjonger.
Description: New York : Crabtree Publishing Company, [2016]
    | Series: Be a maker! | Includes index. | Description based
    on print version record and CIP data provided by publisher;
    resource not viewed.
Identifiers: LCCN 2015046002 (print) | LCCN 2015044050
    (ebook) | ISBN 9781427117205 (electronic HTML) | ISBN
    9780778722526 (reinforced library binding : alk. paper) | ISBN
    9780778722649 (pbk. : alk. paper)
Subjects: LCSH: Musical instruments--Construction--Juvenile
    literature. | Makerspaces--Juvenile literature.
Classification: LCC ML460 (print) | LCC ML460 .S58 2016 (ebook)
    | DDC 784.192/3--dc23
LC record available at http://lccn.loc.gov/2015046002

Crabtree Publishing Company

www.crabtreebooks.com   1-800-387-7650

Printed in Canada/022016/MA20151130

**Published in Canada
Crabtree Publishing**
616 Welland Ave.
St. Catharines, Ontario
L2M 5V6

**Published in the United States
Crabtree Publishing**
PMB 59051
350 Fifth Avenue, 59th Floor
New York, New York 10118

**Published in the United Kingdom
Crabtree Publishing**
Maritime House
Basin Road North, Hove
BN41 1WR

**Published in Australia
Crabtree Publishing**
3 Charles Street
Coburg North
VIC, 3058

CONTENTS

Time to Make!   4
The Science of Sound   6
The Sound of Music   8
Make It! Water Trombone   10
Vibrating Air   12
Vibrating Strings   14
Vibrating Instruments   16
Vibrating Membranes   18
Make It! DIY Drum   20
Vibrating Vocals   22
Electronic Music   24
New Vibrations   26
Make It! Play the Pegboard   28
Glossary   30
Learning More   31
Index   32

TIME TO MAKE!

What do the ancient Greeks and Canadian superstar Deadmau5 have in common? They are both makers! The link is one of the world's most popular ways of making music: keyboard instruments. More than 2,000 years ago, the Greeks invented an organ powered by water. Later makers replaced the water with air to make pipe organs. Skip ahead to today and Deadmau5's prized grand piano. He hooks it up to his computer to make electronic music. Who will design the next advance in keyboards? It could be you!

PIONEERS OF MUSIC

Throughout history, the **pioneers** of music have been creative and resourceful. In ancient Sri Lanka, someone joined a coconut shell and a bamboo stem with a few other everyday objects. It became one of the earliest instruments to be played with a **bow**. People still make music using ordinary items. Take the members of Vienna's Vegetable Orchestra, for example. They make and play vegetable instruments—from carrot flutes to pumpkin drums. Could coconuts or carrots be used in your music projects?

THE MAKER MOVEMENT

People who invent new instruments and ways of performing music are part of a growing group called makers. They are from many different fields, but they have a lot in common.

The design of these *ravanahatha* comes from ancient Sri Lankan coconut-and-bamboo instruments.

4

Makers often collaborate, or work together, in makerspaces and labs. They gather to share tools and knowledge. There might be a makerspace near you.

RISK TAKING

Hands-on experiments are a big part of the maker movement. Makers take risks because they believe they can change the world. Failure will not stop them. They learn from their mistakes and persist until they find solutions. Creative resources and inspiration are everywhere—even in the vegetable aisle of the grocery store!

DESIGN PROCESSES

Some people make their own instruments because they are expensive to buy and repair. Other makers have an instrument they want to adapt. They alter the original design to work in a different way. Music makers bring their ideas to life through a variety of creative processes. They may design by trial-and-error. This process involves trying different approaches until one works well. Often makers start with an idea, develop a **prototype**, test it, and then improve it.

a *cajón*

Be inspired by instruments from around the world! This maker is building a *cajón*, which is a drum from Peru.

THE SCIENCE OF SOUND

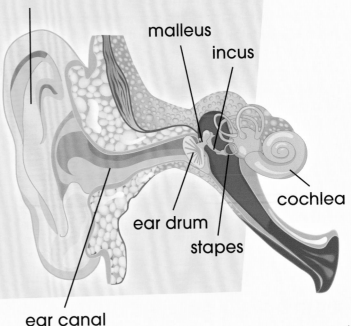

Believe it or not, when makers innovate with music they also experiment with physics. This science explores how energy and **matter** interact. Did you know that sound is actually energy that can be heard?

VIBRATIONS TO SOUND

When Taylor Swift strums her guitar, she causes its strings to vibrate. The matter that surrounds the strings—air in this case—begins to vibrate, too. Vibrations produce **sound waves** that travel in all directions.

HEARING

The outer ear collects sound waves. These waves move through the ear canal and hit the eardrum. Its tightly stretched tissue vibrates like the surface of a drum. Parts in the inner ear pick up the vibrations and send signals to the brain. It interprets them and we hear sounds. If your parents tell you to turn down the music on your headphones, listen to them! Loud sounds can damage the inner ear and cause hearing loss.

outer ear

malleus

incus

cochlea

ear drum

stapes

ear canal

Be a Maker!

After German composer **Ludwig van Beethoven lost his hearing, he sat on the floor and played a legless piano. He could not hear his own music, but he could feel the piano's vibrations through the floor. People who are deaf can enjoy music by touching an instrument while a musician plays it, or feeling vibrations coming from speakers. What could you do to try "feeling" music instead of hearing it? How could senses other than hearing or touch help you to experience music?**

MAKE SOME NOISE

Any object that vibrates creates a sound that could become music. You can try it right now! Clap your hands or stomp your feet to produce vibrations. Tap on a glass or slam a door shut. Grab a pen and drum a beat on a variety of surfaces. The very first instruments began with people using everyday items to make sounds. Challenge yourself to make as many unique sounds as possible with objects you find in your kitchen.

Waves of sound energy move through the air from this *djembe* into listeners' ears.

THE SOUND OF MUSIC

Mixing random sounds together just makes noise. We create music by purposely combining sounds. Understanding a few main sound concepts will help you with making your own music.

PITCH

The speed of vibrations affects sound. Faster vibrations have a higher **pitch**, whereas slower vibrations sound lower. Each musical note links to a pitch. Mariah Carey is famous for her wide **range**, which is the span of notes she can sing. Her range is no match for a pipe organ, though. Each pipe has a different pitch and one organ may have hundreds—or thousands—of pipes!

TIMBRE

What happens if a variety of instruments play the same pitch? They will not sound the same. Our ears pick up subtle differences in the qualities of sound produced by each instrument, known as their **timbre**.

A glockenspiel's metal keys are high-pitched. When making your instrument, experiment with using different materials to alter the pitch.

VOLUME

The intensity or size of sound waves affects volume. The crowd at a Drake concert perceives the vibrations blasting from speakers as having a louder volume. If he whispers to someone onstage, however, the low **intensity** lowers the volume. These sound waves are too quiet for others to hear.

CHANGING VIBRATIONS

When making your own musical instrument, consider how it produces vibrations and if you can modify them. For example, guitar strings have varying thicknesses, which create different pitches. Tightening, loosening, shortening, and lengthening the strings also adjusts their pitch. A guitarist changes notes by pressing down on the strings, which shortens them. The size, shape, and material of a guitar will also affect its timbre.

The design and materials of this double bass give it a very low pitch. Its rich timbre is distinct from other stringed instruments.

Makers and Shakers

Iner Souster

Most people would regard a broken speaker, fridge parts, and an old bowl as trash. Toronto-based musician Iner Souster (born 1971) saw the makings of a large string instrument that he later named the bowafridgeaphone. His first attempt to create the instrument ended in disaster when he pulled a string too tightly and the whole thing fell apart. He did not give up—he just tried again until he was successful. He started making at age 12 when he pieced together old parts he found in his dad's garage. He has made many one-of-a-kind musical instruments since then.

MAKE IT!
WATER TROMBONE

Some instruments produce vibrations by blowing air through a tube. The length and width of the tube determine the pitch. The materials used to make the instrument affect the timbre. The volume changes with the strength of the blowing.

YOU WILL NEED
- A tall drinking glass or bottle
- Water
- A drinking straw

1 ● Fill a glass or bottle with water. While holding the top end of the straw, insert it into the water.

● Line your lips up with the top of the straw so that when you blow, your breath moves across the top opening of the straw. It should produce a sound.

● If you do not hear a sound, change the placement of the straw or try pressing it against your bottom lip.

2

3

- Lower the straw into the water until the top part of the straw is just above the top of the bottle and blow.
- Keep blowing as you slowly raise the straw up through the water.
- Try quickly moving the straw up and down. Notice how the pitch changes.
- Test what happens when you blow softer or harder on the straw.

4

- Now make some music! Create a simple **melody**, which is a series of high and low notes, on your water trombone.

CONCLUSION

- What did you observe about pitch and volume while playing your water trombone?
- How did the pitch change as the amount of air in the straw increased or decreased?
- In what ways did blowing harder or softer change the volume?

Make It Even Better!

Try this activity again. Experiment with using different materials, such as other liquids, or straws with varying diameters and thicknesses. You could also try it with multiple straws cut at different lengths. How do you think changing the materials will affect the pitch or volume of your water trombone?

VIBRATING AIR

Water trombones—and brass trombones—are part of a huge group of instruments that make sounds mainly by vibrating the air inside them.

ONE, TWO, THREE, BLOW!

Many thousands of years ago, people blew air into hollow animal bones to make music. Covering a carved finger hole changed the pitch, just as it does on flutes today. Simple whistles made from bones were another early instrument that relied on vibrating air. They played one note but could increase in volume with stronger blowing.

There are now hundreds of instruments that make sounds by vibrating air. Harmonicas, bagpipes, and even conch shells belong to this diverse group. Along with designs and materials, the way the air is blown, and how strongly, will affect volume and pitch. A player's lips may buzz against a mouthpiece, as with a tuba. Lips may also vibrate directly on an object, such as the opening of a conch shell. Other instruments, including clarinets, involve blowing air over one or more **reeds**, which changes how the air vibrates.

Experiment with vibrating air! What sounds can you produce with a cardboard tube, wind-up siren, or party horn?

If you have a conch shell, try blowing air into it. What sounds can you make by blowing in different ways?

SAX HACKS

Saxophones are less than 200 years old. This makes them new inventions compared to most instruments. They are named after their maker, Adolphe Sax from Belgium, who started making instruments at around age 14. Like many music makers, Sax enjoyed mixing different parts of instruments together. When he put the reed mouthpiece of a clarinet onto a tuba-like brass body, he designed the first saxophone, or sax.

Louis Armstrong is blowing into this trumpet's mouthpiece. The way a trumpeter blows changes how the air vibrates inside the instrument.

Inventive makers will **hack** any instrument —even newer ones like the sax. Angel Sampedro del Rio made the first bamboo sax in 1985. He used trial-and-error to perfect the sax in his family's workshop in Argentina. The final design joins bamboo stems together. It uses traditional reeds but the bamboo body gives the instrument a distinct timbre.

Be a Maker!

This book groups instruments using the Hornbostel-Sachs system. It sorts them by how they produce sounds. You may be more familiar with the Western instrument families: strings, woodwinds, brass, and percussion. This system is helpful for organizing many instruments. However, it leaves out less common instruments, such as didgeridoos. How could learning more about the similarities and differences of each group of instruments help you as a maker?

VIBRATING STRINGS

How many ways can you think of to vibrate the strings of a musical instrument? Here is a hint to start your list: this book already described the way guitars produce sound on page nine. In addition to strumming strings, musicians can pick, pluck, strike, and move a bow across them.

SO MANY STRINGS

The idea to stretch strings tightly to create sounds is ancient. One of the earliest examples is the harp. Egyptians in 3000 BCE used hair or plant fibers as harp strings. Centuries later, lyres were popular string instruments in Greece. Their strings were made of dried sheep intestines! A piece of horn or bone was used to pluck the strings to vibrate them. People still play harps and lyres today. Other modern string instruments include the banjo, cello, and mandolin.

Did you know that vibrating strings also make the sounds inside pianos? Pianists press keys that connect to small hammers. These hammers hit the strings and make them vibrate. Each key plays a different note because each string has its own pitch. Pressing a key softly or powerfully changes the volume of its sound.

Artwork on an ancient Egyptian tomb shows what harps looked like thousands of years ago.

14

Bo Diddley

Bo Diddley (1928–2008) was a maker who ruled rock and roll in the 1950s. Friends used to call him "the junkman" because he made instruments from just about anything. He even filled plastic toilet parts with black-eyed peas to make maracas! His signature creations were rectangular guitars made from old wood and cigar boxes. Diddley did not just invent instruments—he rocked with them. His style still influences music today.

Bo Diddley challenged traditional ways of making music by turning cigar boxes into guitars.

SUPER STRINGS

We have pianos because of Bartolomeo Cristofori. This Italian inventor played about with the design of the **harpsichord** for years. This led to him making the first piano around 1700. At the same time in Italy, Antonio Stradivari and his family were handcrafting string instruments such as violins. Their artistry made them one of the most famous families of makers ever. Just one Stradivarius instrument sells for millions of dollars today!

If Cristofori or Stradivari were around today, they could try new technologies such as **three-dimensional (3-D)** printers. Find out if a library near you has one of these printers. You can watch as it "prints" layers of material such as plastic to create objects from drawings. 3-D printers can even make the bodies of string instruments!

VIBRATING INSTRUMENTS

Strings are not the only part of an instrument that can produce vibrations. One group of instruments vibrate all over their bodies. Depending on the materials used to make them, they can have different pitches or one distinct sound.

Materials used to make instruments change over time. Metal replaced bamboo keys in ancient African thumb pianos.

SHAKE, RATTLE, AND ROLL

The people who created flutes with animal bones also made music by striking or scraping bones together. Using different objects, such as stones or body parts, produced other sounds. These early makers also strung together seeds, shells, and other everyday items to create bracelets and anklets. They rattled when the wearers danced. People also made music with items such as dried gourds (a type of fruit). The **friction** between the outer gourd and the hardened seeds inside it caused sound vibrations. You could make similar musical instruments yourself!

The discovery of metals allowed makers to create sounds that people had never heard before. These instruments were also more durable. Bronze bells that date back about 4,000 years still exist in China. Modern metal instruments in this group include cymbals, triangles, and xylophones.

MAKING OLD THINGS NEW

American inventor Benjamin Franklin tried his hand at making a vibrating instrument in the 1700s. People already knew that moving a wet finger around the rim of a glass creates vibrations and a beautiful sound. Franklin built on that idea. His armonica used dozens of glass bowls that spun as a single unit. In your own music projects, consider how you can use old ideas to make something new!

Vibrating instruments do not require complicated designs like that of Franklin's armonica. Music makers are resourceful. They can produce sounds from almost anything. For example, the musical saw is exactly what you think it is. A musician holds a metal handsaw— very carefully— and pulls a bow across it or taps it with a hammer to create vibrations.

The largest bowls of an armonica produce the lowest pitches, while smaller bowls have higher pitches.

Be a Maker!

Have you noticed that many instruments played today are adapted from older versions of the same instruments? Name some examples. How does the fact that completely new instruments are rare change your approach as a maker? What do centuries of music hacks tell you about the current maker movement?

17

VIBRATING MEMBRANES

Instruments that vibrate relate closely to instruments with vibrating **membranes**. In fact, they are often lumped into one group called percussion instruments. They make sounds differently, however.

MEMBRANE MATERIALS

A vibrating membrane is a tightly stretched material that usually covers the opening of a drum base. The earliest membranes were skins from animals such as elephants and alligators. As they dried, the skins tightened over the openings of hollow clay or wooden frames. Ropes often held the edges of the membranes against drums.

After thousands of years, a new membrane material replaced animal skins. An American chemical company invented the first **synthetic** drumhead in the 1950s. It was more durable and less prone to damage when damp, which was a problem with animal-skin drumheads.

The size, shape, and materials used to make a drum all affect the sounds it makes.

DRUMSTICKS

At first, musicians used their hands to vibrate membranes. Wooden tools fall apart over time, so it is difficult to know who made the first wooden drumsticks. They are at least 1,000 years old, though. Using different drumsticks changes the sound of a drum. The vibrations vary depending on their tip shapes and the woods used to make them.

MODERN INSTRUMENTS

Common drums played today include timpani, bongo, bass, snare, and tom-tom drums. Like earlier drums, modern versions often have wooden bodies, also called shells. Makers also use metals and plastics to create drum bodies. The different materials produce different sounds. The shape and thickness of shells and drumheads also change the timbre.

You can find drum-making inspiration from the prototype created by a team from Yamaha. They began the design process by brainstorming ideas for a drum kit, which is a set of percussion instruments. It needed to include drums, cymbals, and cowbells. They used their best ideas to design and build a prototype.

One drummer stands inside the frame of this prototype drum kit and dances as they play.

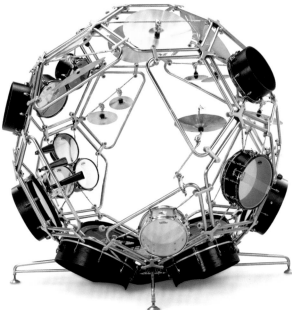

Be a Maker!

Drum kits can produce powerful vibrations. Changing the acoustics **alters their sounds. Acoustics refers to the qualities of a room that affect how sound travels around it and reflects off surfaces. For example, a carpeted floor absorbs vibrations and makes sounds quieter. A great place to intensify vibrations is a small tiled shower! Pay attention to the space in which you make music. How does it affect the sounds you make?**

MAKE IT!
DIY DRUM

Drums have distinct timbres based on their designs and materials. Experiment with materials and sounds by making your own drum!

YOU WILL NEED
- Cylindrical drum body materials, such as cardboard tubes, or empty metal or plastic containers
- Durable drumhead materials, such as balloons, packing tape, or plastic lids
- Materials to attach the drumhead, such as elastic bands, staples, or duct tape
- Scissors

1

- Brainstorm possible supplies for your drum. Consider items for the body that are different sizes and depths and have walls with varying thicknesses. These factors will decide the timbre of the drum, along with the drumhead you use.
- Select one body object and one drumhead material from your list of ideas. Here, the drum body is plastic and the drumhead is packing tape.

- If the drumhead will not stay on with the materials you have selected, experiment with other materials from your brainstorming session. Try different ways of attaching the drumhead. Remember, makers learn from failures instead of quitting when things go wrong.

2

3

- Use your fingers to tap a rhythm on your drum and hear how it sounds. You can adjust it by tightening or loosening the drumhead.

4

- Try out your new drum! See if it sounds any different when played on the ground or held off the floor between your knees. Test the drum in spaces with different acoustics, such as a large, carpeted room or inside your (dry!) bathtub.

CONCLUSION

Observe whether your drum is able to make different sounds. For example, does it change when you strike various spots on the drumhead? Why do you think the size, thickness, and tightness of a drumhead changes the sound of a drum? Reflect on what other materials you would try working with if you did this activity again.

Make It Even Better!

Why stop at one drum when you can make a whole kit? Brainstorm a list of creative resources you could use to make more drums by varying the sizes, shapes, and materials. What are the pros and cons of your ideas?

VIBRATING VOCALS

There is one musical instrument that almost everyone has. It is not the product of brainstorming, prototyping, or testing. People use the original design in a huge variety of ways. It is the human voice! When you speak or sing, air causes two tiny folds in your throat to vibrate. Try humming with your fingers on your throat to feel the vibrations.

Opera is a theatrical form of singing. This kind of vocal music may not be your style, but it has remained popular for over 400 years!

EARLY VOCALS

Evidence suggests that people once sang in the cave areas where the acoustics made their voices sound the best. The sounds of the earliest vocal music are lost to us today. However, history shows that every culture has its own distinctive styles.

Vocal music has many different roots. For example, **yodeling** began in the Alps mountain range as a way to call out to faraway places. It turned into music over hundreds of years. Early choral singing in southern Africa enforced the values of the community. In traditional **throat singing**, Canadian Inuit women usually perform in pairs. They developed it as a pastime while men were off hunting.